MACKINAC ISLAND'S
GRAND HOTEL

Grand Hotel, known as "America's summer place," is perfectly situated on Mackinac Island, known as the "Jewel of the North." The island's location in the Straits of Mackinac is at a point where Lake Huron and Lake Michigan meet. It is known for its pure water-washed air that has cured those suffering from hay fever and respiratory ailments. (Courtesy Bentley Historical Library, University of Michigan.)

MACKINAC ISLAND'S
GRAND HOTEL

MIKE FORNES

ARCADIA
PUBLISHING

Published by Arcadia Publishing
Charleston, South Carolina

Printed in the United States of America

Library of Congress Control Number: 2020952551

For all general information, please contact Arcadia Publishing:
Telephone 843-853-2070
Fax 843-853-0044
E-mail sales@arcadiapublishing.com
For customer service and orders:
Toll-Free 1-888-313-2665

Visit us on the Internet at www.arcadiapublishing.com

Dedicated to those who love the magic of Mackinac Island . . .

CONTENTS

ACKNOWLEDGMENTS

Many thanks are due to those who helped make this telling of Grand Hotel's story possible. First and foremost, the assistance and cooperation of Grand Hotel's staff and management is greatly appreciated in providing the majority of the photographs that appear in this book. Julie Rogers provided access to wonderful color photographs and to the historical archives of the Bentley Historical Library at the University of Michigan, and Sarah Wright located many key items that helped tell the story of the hotel.

Grand Hotel's historian, Bob Tagatz, must be thanked for his perspective on dates and factual clarification that took us back to the 1880s, and Dominick Miller of Mackinac State Historic Parks is appreciated for digging into the park's archives for additional photographs.

The chapter about Grand Hotel's Hollywood connection would not have been complete without the encouragement of Jo Addie and her husband, Jim, who provided key photographs and background about the film *Somewhere in Time* from the archives of their organization, the International Network of *Somewhere in Time* Enthusiasts (INSITE).

Finally, grateful acknowledgment is due to Grand Hotel's group sales staff, who have assisted me in gaining my own firsthand experiences and behind-the-scenes looks during some 30 years of bringing tour groups to the hotel. Julia Luckey-Ottenwess and Corrinne Hamilton have always made me feel like an honored guest at the hotel while allowing me the privilege of showing group tours around, often providing guidance as to what is new and not to be missed. They always helped me look good to our mutual clients, and that is very much appreciated and was so helpful in writing this book.

INTRODUCTION

A Michigan icon, Grand Hotel is in its third century of being known as "America's summer place." The ambiance of Mackinac Island combines with the hotel's ultimate level of hospitality, premier dining, and five-star guest experience for an unforgettable stop on any visitor's itinerary.

Who can resist the clip-clop of horses, the sweet aroma of lilacs, and a soft summer breeze off a cobalt-tinted freshwater sea under equally blue skies and warm sunshine? Not many, it would seem, judging from the return rate of those who visit this classic edifice in its idyllic location.

What a perfect place for a picnic lunch. What a magical place to take a family. Could there be a more romantic setting for a wedding, let alone a honeymoon?

The hotel's aura has been captured by Hollywood on film and relied upon by politicians and the business community for conferences, networking, and relaxation. For more than 85 years, three generations of one family—the Mussers—have inspected each room before the opening of the season and planned constant off-season improvements. Everyday guests are treated with the same welcoming smiles and handshakes that presidents, dignitaries, and celebrities receive.

As of 2020, Grand Hotel offered guests 397 unique rooms—with no two decorated exactly the same. Some of the most exceptional accommodations are the more than 40 Named Rooms. These individualized quarters reflect the lives of several US presidents and first ladies as well as various historical time periods, decorating styles, and prominent figures and events throughout history.

With an unparalleled array of dining options, guests can choose from a full breakfast, the Grand Buffet Luncheon, afternoon tea, and a multicourse dinner in the Main Dining Hall augmented by less formal offerings at the hotel's off-site properties. Sandwiches, salads, seafood, snacks, and ice cream are all available nearby at the Jockey Club, the Woods Restaurant, or Sadie's Ice Cream Parlor, plus other off-property eateries.

Many workout options are available to keep off any extra pounds. Golf, tennis, duckpin bowling, bicycling, a swimming pool, and an outdoor exercise course are encouraged for guests to use.

Grand Hotel has been named a National Historic Landmark and was added to the National Register of Historic Places in 1970.

The hotel's new ownership has resolved to maintain traditions, quality of service, and the constants that make Grand Hotel so impressive. Three generations of the Musser family have charted the course to continue the hotel's impressive legacy.

The following pages are intended to take the reader up the red carpeted steps, through the doors, back to the past, behind the scenes, and into today's world of Mackinac Island finery.

One

FIRST IMPRESSIONS

By 1886, Mackinac Island had already begun earning a reputation as a summer getaway for elite tourists. Most arrived by steamship, but accommodations on the island itself were very limited. To further establish a destination for travelers, the Michigan Central Railroad, Grand Rapids & Indiana Railroad, and Detroit and Cleveland Steamship Navigation Company formed the Mackinac Island Hotel Company to provide first-class lodging for their passengers in a magnificent hotel.

The hotel's foundation was laid in the fall of 1886. Construction, which involved nearly two million feet of white pine milled in St. Ignace and hauled across the ice from the mainland, began in 1887. Charles W. Caskey's crew of nearly 600 workers was hired to build the 200-room wood-frame structure and completed the project in 93 days. The laborers lived in tents near the construction site and worked in three shifts. A classic style was chosen, with columns on a long front porch that the company felt would still look good in 100 years.

Gradually, more additions to the hotel enlarged its overall footprint, and wings on the east and west ends provided a more rounded, finished image. More rooms, more amenities and classic decor, upgrades, and landscaping crafted the hotel's look into more of what can be seen today.

Nearby farmland became a golf course. A 500,000-gallon swimming pool was added. Various other properties were acquired and developed into additional restaurants and lodging. Internally, the hotel retained its 19th-century charm, but behind the scenes, technology was gradually added and infrastructure reinforced and modernized.

Grand Hotel evolved through the years but has always been the perfect summer place.

Mackinac Island was beginning to be known as a summer getaway prior to 1886, but accommodations in the area were always limited. The Michigan Central Railroad, Grand Rapids & Indiana Railroad, and Detroit and Cleveland Steamship Navigation Company then formed the Mackinac Island Hotel Company to build a destination hotel for their transportation interests. Land was purchased from Michigan legislator Francis B. Stockbridge, who had dreamed of building a hotel, and a design by the Detroit architectural firm of Mason & Rice was chosen. Cadotte Avenue, as yet unpaved, could be a dusty or muddy walkway to Plank's Grand Hotel, as it was first known. Rates ranged from $3 to $5 per night when it opened on July 10, 1887. The hotel's west wing was added in 1897. (Courtesy Bentley Historical Library, University of Michigan.)

The surname of John Oliver Plank, Grand Hotel's first manager, was soon removed from the name of Mackinac Island's new showplace. Mark Twain lectured in the hotel's casino in 1895 for a $1 admission fee. In 1910, the hotel was purchased by Henry Weaver, who had been its manager since 1900. The new manager, James "The Comet" Hayes, invited an agent of Edison Phonograph to conduct regular demonstrations of the new invention. A sidewalk was added to allow for better pedestrian passage aside the horse-and-carriage route up the hill. (Courtesy Grand Hotel.)

The land in front of the hotel, where cattle were kept, was a pasture owned by Fort Mackinac. In 1901, this area was developed into the front nine holes of the Jewel Golf Course. The hotel was sold again in 1918, this time to J. Logan Ballard, who died only five years later. (Courtesy Bentley Historical Library, University of Michigan.)

In this photograph, the east end of the hotel has yet to be added, but the walkway to the front lawn is in place. Note the dormers in the hotel's roofline, a feature only recently returned to the overall design of the top floor. The iconic cupola at the building's highest point became the Cupola Bar in 1987. (Courtesy Bentley Historical Library, University of Michigan.)

This image shows the east end addition completed, streetlights added to Cadotte Avenue, and more landscaping underway on the hotel grounds. In 1925, William Stewart Woodfill purchased the hotel along with two other men to whom he later sold his shares. In 1933, Woodfill again purchased the hotel, this time as sole owner, after it fell into receivership. Woodfill, who also managed the hotel for a number of years, retained ownership throughout the mid-20th century, though he gradually turned over responsibility for the hotel's management to his nephew, R.D. "Daniel" Musser II, beginning in 1951. (Courtesy Bentley Historical Library, University of Michigan.)

A gathering of carriages is pictured at the hotel's east end, which is not yet completed in this vintage photograph. Today, Grand Hotel's carriages and taxis drop off guests and pick them up at the main front entrance, and the east end entrance is used for group tours with multiple carriages. Arrival at Grand Hotel has always been by horse-drawn carriage. Automobiles have been banned from Mackinac Island since 1898, when Thomas Chambers successfully petitioned the village council to ban the "horseless carriages" that startled the horses. The law was not strictly enforced until the 1930s. (Courtesy Bentley Historical Library, University of Michigan.)

This gentleman, out with his lady for an evening ride, posed for a photograph on the hotel's driveway, which was still unpaved. The front porch's original portico is visible at the main entrance. The lady is riding sidesaddle, which was customary at the time. The hotel offered horseback-riding lessons in its early days as well as bicycle-riding lessons when bicycles became popular. (Courtesy Bentley Historical Library, University of Michigan.)

The front porch has always been a popular gathering place for guests at Grand Hotel. Parties, receptions, news conferences, and informal get-togethers can draw crowds of various types and sizes, as shown in these vintage photographs. The above photograph, taken from the east, features a considerably larger group than the below photograph looking from the west. (Both, courtesy Bentley Historical Library, University of Michigan.)

These stone gateposts and shrubbery flanked the sidewalk entrance on the east end of the hotel for many years—into the 1940s—but were later removed. This is the location where uniformed ladies now greet pedestrians who are approaching the hotel to ask if they would like to register as a guest, visit the porch, or enjoy the buffet luncheon or afternoon tea. An identical set of stone gateposts were still in place at the hotel's west entrance as of 2020. (Both, courtesy Bentley Historical Library, University of Michigan.)

As Grand Hotel began to modernize in the mid-1900s, entryways were enlarged for carriage traffic, and shrubbery was removed from in front of the ground-floor windows, allowing for a gorgeous view of the grounds and the Straits of Mackinac. The east entrance of Grand Hotel, pictured here, is where guests can access the ground-floor shops and stroll the hallway to the registration desk. Group tours enter and exit here when using multiple taxis or carriages for an island tour. (Courtesy Grand Hotel.)

This longways view from the mid-1900s shows many chaise lounge chairs for relaxing and table settings along its 660-foot length. At this time, the world's longest front porch was outfitted with more relaxing furniture. One edition of *Ripley's Believe It or Not!* incorrectly listed the porch's length as 20 feet longer, at 680 feet. (Courtesy Bentley Historical Library, University of Michigan.)

The classic arrival at Grand Hotel is by omnibus carriage drawn by a team of Percheron horses up Cadotte Avenue from Mackinac Island's downtown area. Hackneys and Belgians also have assignments on the island working carriage tours and pulling drays. The omnibus carriage, which was recently reconditioned in Indiana, has been restored to its original glory. Note the light blue color painted on the undersides of the balconies and porch roof. The signature Grand Hotel blue paint color is "Dew Kiss," manufactured by PPG Pittsburgh Paints. The color discourages birds from nesting there, as they are fooled into thinking it is the open sky above. (Both, courtesy Grand Hotel.)

Two

FLORA AND FAUNA

The same painstaking attention to detail that is evident in the hotel's room decor, dining experiences, and hospitality is also very much a part of Grand Hotel's garden display. The designs, planning, planting, cultivation, and harvest of the many plants and flowers on the grounds is an extensive operation. More than 125,000 annuals are used in this process. Flowers that even hint at wilting or discoloration are immediately replaced with glorious fresh blooms. An extensive greenhouse is maintained for the ongoing purpose of growing new flowers.

Grand Hotel's gardens have evolved over the years. Carefully sculpted shrubbery and paved walkways have given way to more open space for recreation. Blank hillsides with anonymous wild growth have been transformed into wildflower areas with milkweed designed to attract monarch butterflies that visit Mackinac Island during their annual migration from Canada and the northern United States to California and Mexico for the winter.

More than simple decoration, the gardens have become part of the hotel's architecture. Flower boxes, hedge sculptures, and strategic planting designs welcome visitors to the hotel's entrance on Cadotte Avenue and enhance guests' visits through sight and scent. Few olfactory sensations match those that can be experienced while visiting Grand Hotel's grounds during Lilac Time in June on a sunny, windless day.

The greenhouse on Grand Hotel's grounds provides a perfect climate for growing flowers for use in various locations on the property. Flowers are watered, cultivated, and grown here until they are ready for transplanting. For well more than a century, the legendary Grand Hotel gardens have provided beautiful visual enhancement to the guest experience. During any one visit, guests can see more than 150 varieties of flowers, including geranium, rose, peony, coleus, garden heliotrope, cosmos, lily, daisy, and begonia. These geraniums and petunias appear ready for transplanting from the greenhouse to flower boxes. (Both, courtesy Grand Hotel.)

A full house of mature flowers is a common sight in season, when a staff of seven full-time gardeners vigilantly watches for needed replacements. As soon as any sign of wilting is noticed, fresh flowers are brought in and replanted. Geraniums entered as one of the hotel's main floral themes in the 1920s and have never left. The 260 porch flower boxes—filled with seven tons of soil and 2,500 geraniums—provide a perfect accent for guests whether they're relaxing in the rocking chairs or arriving or departing in a carriage. Three thousand more are planted in the ground, totaling more than 5,500 geraniums used in all flower beds. (Both, courtesy Grand Hotel.)

As May turns to June, tulips become the stars of the gardening team. Every October, 25,000 tulip bulbs are planted, and all of them come from Holland—Holland, Michigan, that is. The Dutch-influenced community, noted for its annual tulip festival and tulip-growing fields, provides Grand Hotel's entire tulip supply. When the flowering is over, all 25,000 bulbs are dug up and thrown away, to be replaced again in the fall for blooming in spring. (Both, courtesy Grand Hotel.)

Of all flowers grown on Mackinac Island and at Grand Hotel, lilacs have a personality and presence all their own. Each June, Lilac Time is the occasion of a downtown parade and many special events to celebrate the blooming of the lavender-colored plant with its sweet, haunting fragrance. This scene is from the area just outside the Esther Williams Swimming Pool. (Courtesy Grand Hotel.)

This horse and carriage topiary, located at the base of the east end of the slope in front of the hotel, is visible from the walkway off Cadotte Avenue that leads to Grand Hotel's driveway, and visitors sometimes do a double-take when seeing the two Hackneys drawing a carriage in the mist or during twilight. The frame is built in horizontal layers, with one layer covered in a netting of fishing line with florist moss pressed into it. Three inches of soil hold individual ivy plants that are planted sideways in the breaks between the moss, and bags of Styrofoam peanuts fill the horses' bellies. Stella D'Oro daylilies comprise the manes and tails. (Courtesy Grand Hotel.)

The Secret Garden is located on the east side of the hotel grounds, north of the tennis courts. A restful and peaceful location, this area has been decorated in different ways accenting a small bridge through flowing floral color schemes that include 2,500 daffodils complemented by hyacinth, anemones, and vinca in purple, pink, blue, and white. In this perfect place for a marriage proposal, nearby benches allow for guests to contemplate the beauty and tranquility of the Secret Garden, which is shown here in spring (above) and summer (below). (Both, courtesy Grand Hotel.)

The perfect setting for an island wedding, the Grand Hotel Tea Garden is fully equipped as a location with built-in scenery. The fountain and many flowers, shrubs, and trees serve as a natural backdrop for summer nuptials. Grand Hotel hosts weddings with as many as 400 guests; during the summer, there can be as many as 20 weddings per day on the island. (Courtesy Grand Hotel.)

The hotel's grounds offer a serene, beautiful setting with ambient light from sunset still present as late as 10:00 p.m. in the month of June. The sweet scent of lilacs in the gardens completes a beautiful Straits of Mackinac evening as a ferryboat heads toward the Mackinac Bridge and the mainland. (Courtesy Grand Hotel.)

Fall colors designate a very special time on Mackinac Island with shorter days and cooler nights. Birch, ash, and white pine trees accent the natural greens of the island's fir and pine foliage. Grand Hotel customarily remains open through the month of October. The island has fewer than 600 year-round residents, most of whom spend long hours working through the summer tourist season that begins to wind down with the onset of autumn. (Courtesy Grand Hotel.)

Three

GRAND AMENITIES

After guests arrive at Grand Hotel, a whole world of amenities awaits those looking for the perfect facility for their activities. From casual outdoor lawn and porch events to business meeting spaces to entertaining taverns and pubs, there is more variety on the hotel's grounds at Mackinac Island than would be found at most convention centers in an urban setting. More than 22,000 square feet of meeting space are augmented by the hotel staff's personal attention to aid in transportation and island logistics, food and beverages, and guest room reservations.

With an established tradition of more than 130 years as the perfect gathering place for business leaders, Grand Hotel offers many unique indoor and outdoor locations ranging from those featuring first-class dining to more casual off-site restaurants for meals and cocktail receptions. Many organizations have returned year after year—some for decades—to hold their annual meetings.

The front lawn of Grand Hotel has been configured in a number of ways over the years and continues to evolve to suit current needs. The space encompasses plenty of room for lawn chair settings, tents to house food and beverage stations, and staging areas for corporate gatherings. Events can be arranged to fit particular spaces ranging from the traditional lines of the Grand Hotel Tea Garden to the more casual environment of the pool area. (Both, courtesy Bentley Historical Library, University of Michigan.)

The Grand Hotel Tea Garden offers flexibility for gatherings as varied as weddings, corporate functions, and convention ceremonies. Because outdoor events are always subject to weather conditions, a backup plan is usually coordinated to involve the theater when necessary. The grounds have evolved over the years to change the landscaping and placement of lawn fixtures. Grand Hotel offers many options and can host wedding ceremonies for up to 400 guests. For many years, the Knights of Columbus convention attracted a large delegation that returned annually for the group's meetings and activities. (Courtesy Bentley Historical Library, University of Michigan.)

A favorite pastime of Grand Hotel guests is to relax in the rocking chairs on the front porch. The rockers, each with a beautiful view of the Straits of Mackinac, are offset by incidental tables and attended by bar service. Young vendors can often be spotted driving bicycle carts on the porch with a cooler of soft drinks available for purchase. (Courtesy Grand Hotel.)

Chess can be played on the front porch with giant game pieces. A chess match can be played discreetly but sometimes attracts a crowd of advisors, one of whom might challenge the winner to the next game. This is an enticing way to introduce children to the game, with onlookers often serving as teachers in strategic theories. (Courtesy Grand Hotel.)

The omnibus carriage transports Grand Hotel guests to and from the ferry docks downtown, as does the taxi service. The vintage carriage offers visitors a chance to return to an earlier era, when the Gilded Age provided luxury service to the elite population of major cities. Horse-drawn taxi service is also available to the hotel from the downtown ferry docks, charging a similar fee. Luggage is transported by horse-drawn dray to and from the docks to the hotel, and guests do not have to handle bags until they are at the hotel or back on the mainland after their ferryboat ride. (Courtesy Grand Hotel.)

In the opening days of Grand Hotel, this greeting spot was viewed with all the grandeur deserving of an island showcase resort for the elite traveler. In modern times, the red-carpeted staircase is where most guests arriving at the hotel pose for a picture before completing registration and entering the hotel's main doors. These steps, shown here in a view from the top, have been climbed by many famous entertainers, politicians, sports figures, and world-famous business leaders in addition to the families who return to Grand Hotel year after year. The hotel welcomed its 5,000,000th guest in 2006, with many more to arrive by private aircraft, ferryboat, horse-drawn carriage, or bicycle to walk up these red-carpeted steps to "America's summer place." The bellman's stand is located at street level, where the omnibus carriage and taxis arrive with guests. However, check-in takes place just around the corner. An elevator is available next to the front desk as well. The red carpeting is replaced each spring, ensuring a fresh start to each season. (Courtesy Grand Hotel.)

Much has changed over the years in the decor and amenities of the ground-floor lobby. The east end offers an entrance easily accessible to group carriage tours. Many shops and food and beverage choices have been added since this 1970s-era photograph was taken. (Courtesy Bentley Historical Library, University of Michigan.)

The hotel's registration desk is pictured when it was located on the parlor level. A new desk (shown below) was established in the downstairs lobby in the 1970s. (Courtesy Grand Hotel.)

The hotel's front desk for check-in is on the ground floor; it was moved from the first-floor parlor level decades ago. Individual and group registrations can be handled by clerks who come to Mackinac Island from around the world. This photograph, taken during the 2020 COVID-19 pandemic, shows protections in place for guests and hotel personnel. (Author's collection.)

Furniture, carpeting, and designs have changed over the years in Grand Hotel's first-floor parlor. Note the differences with regard to tables, sofas, and overhead lighting, plus three different carpeting designs. Also visible in these photographs from the late 20th century are ashtrays, which indicate that it was the end of an era when smoking was permitted in the hotel. (Both, courtesy Bentley Historical Library, University of Michigan.)

The colorful modern-day parlor offers seating for guests waiting to enter the Main Dining Hall or those lounging with a book to read, and it also serves as a gathering place for those setting out on a Mackinac Island adventure. This area was formerly the location of the lobby; however, guests now register one level below, on the ground floor. (Courtesy Grand Hotel.)

The entrance to the Terrace Room is a comfortable place to sit just off the main parlor. As in other parlor locations, the decor has evolved over the years but has always been furnished in soft, plush textures and rich fabrics. (Courtesy Grand Hotel.)

The Terrace Room is a lively place on most any evening for guests seeking a nightclub atmosphere. Entertainment and dancing are typical fare, with the Grand Hotel Orchestra often on stage. (Courtesy Bentley Historical Library, University of Michigan.)

Grand Hotel's theater was built to accommodate events ranging from meetings, conventions, and trade shows to dinners with entertainment and ballroom dancing. This 1900s-era gathering appears to be businessmen at an annual get-together. Note the spittoons, which were commonly in use at the time. (Courtesy Bentley Historical Library, University of Michigan.)

This mid-20th-century assembly appears to bring together representatives of all the states, judging by the collection of flags on stage. Grand Hotel has always been the perfect choice for a mid-America meeting away from the hustle and bustle of a big city. (Courtesy Bentley Historical Library, University of Michigan.)

A typical trade show configuration allows for plenty of foot traffic passing vendor displays. The patterns are designed to keep attendees moving logically and allow them to see all the vendors with equal visibility. (Courtesy Bentley Historical Library, University of Michigan.)

The theater has been arranged in a seminar format for this event, with a head table for speakers and one presenter's position. The business capabilities of Grand Hotel are every bit as versatile as those designed for entertainment activities. This arrangement is set for approximately 100 attendees as well as presenters. (Courtesy Bentley Historical Library, University of Michigan.)

The Grand Hotel Theatre is shown here in a completely different configuration, designed for a wedding with a dais on stage. Seating can vary, with more place settings available on the sides of the room if necessary. A business dinner group could use a similar setup with a keynote speaker at the dais. (Courtesy Bentley Historical Library, University of Michigan.)

A dinner show at the Grand Hotel Theatre can comfortably seat 300 guests with good visibility of the stage show. This setup, likely for a party of 200 guests, permits generous spacing for servers with an onstage dais and grand piano. A dinner event with a dance floor and stage show can be easily accomplished by the Grand Hotel Theatre staff. Rectangular tables allow for a larger number of guests and the inclusion of a dance floor. The stage is accessed from the wings, allowing for unobstructed entry for performers. (Courtesy Bentley Historical Library, University of Michigan.)

The Carousel Bar, shown here in the 1960s, featured refreshments ranging from cold lemonade to cocktails. Note the decorative equine theme, which is popular on Mackinac Island, the home of 500 summer horses. Besides horses, turtles are a common symbol of the island. Native Americans referred to Mackinac Island as "Land of the Great Turtle" due to its distinctive shape as it appears when viewed from St. Ignace. The natives of this sacred place referred to it as *Michinnimackinong*, which the French translated to *Michilimackinac*, and it was eventually shortened to Mackinac, which is still the name of the island and the southern tip of the Upper Peninsula. The British Anglicized the word to Mackinaw, which today refers only to the Mackinaw City area. Both words are pronounced with an "aw" ending. (Courtesy Grand Hotel.)

The Geranium Bar is located just off the main parlor near the entrance to the Main Dining Hall and the world's longest front porch. Over the years, it became known as the perfect place to meet for pre-dinner cocktails. The black-and-white checkered floor supports delicate red lacquer chairs covered in rich fabrics. If one prefers to enjoy a drink on the porch, service to the white rocking chairs is available from the Geranium Bar. (Courtesy Grand Hotel.)

The Audubon Wine Bar is located just off the main parlor, across from the staircase that leads down to the ground-floor lobby. A classy lounging area with comfortable furnishings, the Audubon serves a complete selection of Michigan's and Napa Valley's finest wines. In addition to its library-like shelving of leather-bound books, a number of classic games are also available. Libations include Highland single-malt scotches, Kentucky's finest bourbons, Polish and Russian vodkas, and France's best cognacs, cordials, and champagnes. Broadcasts of popular sporting events are often watched here. This area of the hotel was formerly a dress shop. During Prohibition, alcohol was smuggled in from Canada, which is 35 miles away by boat, and hidden in the sewing room. (Courtesy Grand Hotel.)

The Jockey Club is located across Cadotte Avenue at the first tee of the Jewel Golf Course. Originally known as the Snack Bar, it was designed as a quick stop for golfers. Outdoor seating is also available, with a tented enclosure during cooler times and heaters placed at various locations throughout the dining area. (Courtesy Grand Hotel.)

The Snack Bar has evolved into more of a country-club setting, as sandwiches and salads are on the luncheon menu before or after a round of golf, and a full dinner is available at night. Beverages ranging from soft drinks to champagne are available for golfers celebrating a round or for the general public. (Courtesy Bentley Historical Library, University of Michigan.)

Surrounded by windows, the Cupola Bar was added to an observation deck on the top floor of Grand Hotel in 1987. It is the perfect spot to enjoy a classic cocktail with live music, as it offers panoramic views of Mackinac Island, Round Island Lighthouse, the Straits of Mackinac, the Mackinac Bridge, and ships heading through Round Island Passage. Sunset is the perfect cocktail hour at the Cupola Bar. (Both, courtesy Grand Hotel.)

An impressive view from the inner railing of the upper level of the Cupola Bar looks down toward the bar's chandelier. An example of Venetian art glass, it hangs above the lower level of the bar and strikes an incredible mood of elegance. It is equally stunning to view it while looking up from the bar's lower level. (Courtesy Grand Hotel.)

The remodeled version of the Cupola Bar includes large windows and bright decor. Guests enjoy a perspective much higher in elevation than the one on the front porch. Casual attire is welcome. An evening's entertainment can vary from a disc jockey spinning tunes to a piano player taking requests from an intimate audience. (Courtesy Grand Hotel.)

Four

THE ROOM *IS* THE VIEW

Hosting more than 150,000 overnight guests each season is not a task Grand Hotel takes lightly. Among the 397 guest rooms (in 2020), some of its most exceptional accommodations are the more than 40 Named Rooms. These unique guest rooms reflect the lives of several US presidents and first ladies, various time periods spanning two centuries, myriad decorating styles, and prominent historical figures and events.

In addition to the suites pictured in this chapter, the hotel also has other Named Rooms available, each featuring their own thematic design, furnishings, and ambiance. As of 2020, those include the China Suite, Commodore Suite, Dorothy Draper Suite, Esther Williams Suite, Founders Suite, Garden Suite, Grand Suite, Hollywood Suite, Huron Suite, Jane Seymour Suite, *Somewhere in Time* Suite, Josephine Suite, Lady Astor Suite, Lilac Suite, Lord Astor Suite, Mackinac Suite, Napoleon Suite, Prentiss M. Brown Suite, Stockbridge Suite, Tiffany Suite, Vanderbilt Suite, Versailles Suite, Victorian Suite, Wicker Suite, Woodfill Suite, Daniel Musser Suite, and others.

Suites honoring US presidents and first ladies as of 2020 include the Lodge of Teddy Roosevelt, Lincoln Suite, Jefferson Suite, Eisenhower Suite, Dolley Madison Suite, Laura Bush Suite, Barbara Bush Suite, Jacqueline Kennedy Suite, Betty Ford Suite, Nancy Reagan Suite, Rosalynn Carter Suite, and Lady Bird Johnson Suite.

A project started in 2014 added 24 dormers to the hotel's roofline. The completion of the Cupola Suites in 2019 brought the hotel's front face back to the way it looked in the 1800s and as late as 1915.

This black-and-white photograph of Grand Hotel's Lincoln Suite far surpasses the early elegance the hotel would become known for. The simple draperies invite guests to peek outside for a magnificent view of the Straits of Mackinac. The authentic 1840s/1850s ornate headboard and bed frame are accompanied by a four-place table setting. By 1919, the rate had increased to $6 per person per day. (Courtesy Bentley Historical Library, University of Michigan.)

By the middle of the 20th century, the hotel's furniture designs varied from comfortable traditional to minimalist with clean lines. Low-profile sofas and chairs were common along with furniture inspired by the Space Age, such as the cone-based coffee table. (Courtesy Bentley Historical Library, University of Michigan.)

Mackinac Island's fresh summer breezes blended well with the upscale decor being added to guest rooms during refurbishing at the turn of the 21st century. However, air-conditioning was not added to the final 170 rooms until 2007, completing a project to air-condition the entire hotel in time for its 120th birthday. During an island power outage that lasted for nearly two weeks in July 2000 (due to an anchor strike that disabled several submerged power cables), huge generators were brought in to provide electricity for basic necessities, including ice, lighting, kitchen equipment, and credit-card machines. (Both, courtesy Grand Hotel.)

One of America's best known interior designers, Carleton Varney, designed Grand Hotel's interior locations and guest rooms from 1976 to 2019 with the adventurous use of vibrant colors, floral patterns, and bold contrasts. Known as "Mr. Color," Varney owns Dorothy Draper & Co., which has a design philosophy that stresses "the use of bright colors and the rejection of all that is impractical, uncomfortable and drab." He also operated Carleton's Tea Store on the hotel's ground-floor level. Varney's influence is apparent in the decor of the Named Rooms featured in this chapter. (Courtesy Dorothy Draper & Co.)

The Vanderbilt Suite, added in 2000, is an excellent example of Carleton Varney's use of color and fabrics. William Henry Vanderbilt, son of railroad magnate Cornelius Vanderbilt, was president of the Michigan Central Railroad, which played a key role in getting Grand Hotel built in 1887. He was also known as a horseman who coached and raced horses. (Courtesy Grand Hotel.)

The Milliken Suite is named for William Grawn Milliken, Michigan's 44th governor. He was the longest-serving governor in Michigan history, remaining in office for more than three four-year terms, from 1969 to 1983. A native of Traverse City, Michigan, Milliken was a graduate of Yale University and served in the US Army Air Forces in World War II. The Milliken Suite encompasses rooms 290, 291, and 292 in the hotel's east end, overlooking the golf course. (Courtesy Grand Hotel.)

The Royal Suite has an exquisitely feminine touch to its decor, with bright shades of pink and white as the main color scheme. The wallpaper and draperies also express these tones. The bright blue carpeting is accented by color-coordinated pillows on the bed and settee. An old-fashioned dressing table completes the fashionable ensemble. (Courtesy Grand Hotel.)

The Musser Suite is a tribute to Daniel and Amelia Musser, who owned the hotel from 1979 until 2013. This one-bedroom suite, added in 2014, is at the west end of the hotel's fourth floor and features an entryway with a wet bar. Steps up to the right lead into a large parlor with a view of the Straits of Mackinac and the Mackinac Bridge. To the left of the entryway is the bedroom with a dormer sitting area. This is one of the newer Cupola Suites—the latest additions to the hotel. (Both, courtesy Grand Hotel.)

In 2015, two additional suites—four bedrooms and two parlors—were added to the west end of the fourth floor. Their completion brought the total number of dormers to 10. The Bali Ha'i Suite is shown below, adding a refreshing ensemble of deep blue sea colors that perfectly blend with the nautical atmosphere just outside the fourth-floor windows. The suite added several four-poster beds with vibrant shades and exciting uses of space. It is often selected as a perfect choice for families. (Both, courtesy Grand Hotel.)

Other family-oriented suites are also decorated in nautical themes, but no two are the same. This is true of all the rooms at Grand Hotel—no two rooms are decorated exactly alike. Carleton Varney's refreshing designs added a variety of color schemes and decor patterns. Some, like the Song of the Islands Suite, emphasize bright sunny splashes of lighter pastel shades, and others have darker, warmer combinations. Especially inviting are the sitting areas at the cupola windows, just three steps up from the bedroom or parlor floor of the suite. Only the Cupola Bar is higher in elevation, affording a million-dollar view of the Straits of Mackinac in front of the hotel. (Both, courtesy Grand Hotel.)

In all, 24 dormers were added to the hotel's roofline during the project that started in 2014. Grand Hotel president Dan Musser III and his father discussed the Cupola Suites project for many years. The completion of the Cupola Suites in 2019 brought the hotel's front face back to the way it looked in the 1800s and as late as 1915. The construction utilized attic space formerly used for storage and transformed it into beautiful, luxuriously decorated suites. These unique accommodations offer flexibility with one- or two-bedroom options with a parlor, which makes them ideal for families or those needing extra space. (Both, courtesy Grand Hotel.)

The Presidential Suite offers this outstanding balcony view from the east end of the hotel. It is impressive whether the time of day is sunrise, midday, or sunset, and the arrival and departure of horse-driven carriages blends with the peaceful scents of the gardens and the ambiance of Mackinac Island life. Below the balcony is the world's longest front porch, 660 feet in length. Beginning in the early 20th century, several presidents were invited to consider Mackinac Island as a location for a summer White House. Among those who declined an opportunity to visit and see for themselves were Calvin Coolidge and Dwight Eisenhower. Ulysses S. Grant did visit the island shortly after the Civil War, but this was long before Grand Hotel was built. (Courtesy Grand Hotel.)

Presidents of the United States are displayed as part of the decor of the Presidential Suite. From room to room, discoveries await in the published works and wall hangings of various commanders in chief. As of 2020, six men who became president—Joe Biden, Bill Clinton, George H.W. Bush, Gerald Ford, John F. Kennedy, and Harry Truman—have visited Grand Hotel. As of 2020, Ford was the only one who visited while in office. Both Bush and Truman arrived after their presidencies, and the three others were US senators prior to their elections to the nation's highest office. Clinton visited while he was governor of Arkansas. (Both, courtesy Grand Hotel.)

The Lincoln Suite is an original in the Named Rooms series. Although Abraham Lincoln died before Grand Hotel was built, he did come very close to Mackinac Island on one occasion before he was elected president. In October 1848, while he was a member of the House of Representatives, Lincoln traveled from Washington, DC, to Springfield, Illinois. Sailing aboard the side-wheel steamer *Globe*, Lincoln passed through the Straits of Mackinac. As president, he later signed an appropriation to finance construction of several Great Lakes lighthouses, including the Old Mackinac Point Lighthouse in Mackinaw City. (Courtesy Grand Hotel.)

The Lodge of Teddy Roosevelt, another original dedicated to a US president, has perhaps the most unusual decor of any room at Grand Hotel. There are several sets of antlers and horns mounted on the walls, and the elegant rustic furniture and green wallpaper lend an outdoorsy feel that is quite comfortable and not "roughing it" at all. The nation's 26th president took office at the age of 42 in 1901 following the assassination of Pres. William McKinley. He was born into a wealthy New York family, but his image as a hunter, conservationist, and leader of the Rough Riders is well portrayed in this suite. "Speak softly and carry a big stick." (Courtesy Grand Hotel.)

The Jefferson Suite is named for the nation's third president, Thomas Jefferson. He was one of America's founding fathers and loved architecture and fine wines. Jefferson would have loved Grand Hotel. The suite named for him is notable for its huge four-poster bed and its red color scheme, which is found in the draperies, wall coverings, and bed skirting. The basic Early American furniture of the bedroom fits well with Jefferson's time period. (Courtesy Grand Hotel.)

The Prentiss M. Brown Suite was designed in honor of the former US senator from St. Ignace. This themed room features the desk the Michigan senator actually used during his time in office. Brown is also the grandfather of Marlee Brown, wife of hotel chairman Daniel Musser III, and is considered to be the "father" of the Mackinac Bridge. Musser's uncle and former Grand Hotel owner Stewart Woodfill worked on the Mackinac Bridge project with Brown. The bibliotheque wallpaper is lined with historic photographs highlighting the life and achievements of Prentiss M. Brown. (Courtesy Grand Hotel.)

Dolley Todd Madison has the distinction of having the first suite at Grand Hotel named for the wife of a US president. For half a century, she was the most important woman in the social circles of America. After her first husband, lawyer John Todd Jr., died in the yellow fever epidemic of 1793, Dolley married James Madison, 17 years her senior, in 1794. She remained happily married to him until his death in 1836. The suite bears several portraits of her and is decorated in rich fabrics and textures befitting her acclaimed social graces and political acumen. (Courtesy Grand Hotel.)

In 1998, five new Named Rooms were added to the west end of the hotel to honor First Ladies Lady Bird Johnson, Betty Ford, Rosalynn Carter, Nancy Reagan, and Barbara Bush. Elizabeth Anne "Betty" Ford was the wife of Pres. Gerald Ford. As First Lady, she was active in social policy and set a precedent as a politically active presidential spouse. She also served as Second Lady of the United States from 1973 to 1974. The suite is decorated in shades of pale green and blue, with bright red carpeting that bears circles of white stars. (Courtesy Grand Hotel.)

First Lady Claudia Alta "Lady Bird" Johnson got her nickname from an aunt who said she was "as pretty as a lady bird." Lady Bird's mother died when she was just five years old, and her aunt came to care for her. Reminiscent of some of the most beautiful natural colors from the state of Texas, the suite is decorated in goldenrod yellow and bluebonnet blue, with circles of white stars in the deep blue carpeting. (Both, courtesy Grand Hotel.)

The deep reds of the Nancy Reagan Suite extend from the bed comforters to the wall colors and the window treatments. An actress in many films, the former Nancy Davis became the second wife of actor Ronald Reagan, who was elected president in 1980. Born Anne Frances Robbins in New York City, she worked as an actress on Broadway before moving to Hollywood to enter the film industry, where she met her husband. As First Lady, she supported veterans, the elderly, and the emotionally and physically handicapped. Nancy Reagan is perhaps best remembered for her passionate advocacy for decreasing drug and alcohol abuse. (Courtesy Grand Hotel.)

Rosalynn Carter, wife of the 39th president of the United States, Jimmy Carter, has a suite decorated in shades of pink and blue, including a deep blue carpet with a circle of white stars at the foot of the bed. During her time as First Lady, from 1977 to 1981, she was an envoy abroad and a leading advocate for numerous causes, including mental health research. Born Eleanor Rosalynn Smith in Plains, Georgia, she focused national attention on the performing arts and invited leading classical artists and traditional American artists to the White House. (Both, courtesy Grand Hotel.)

The Barbara Bush Suite, named for the wife of the nation's 41st president, George H.W. Bush, has a very relaxing combination of light blue, white, and gold colors. An impressive portrait of Barbara Bush is a central focus of the room's decor. After serving as Second Lady from 1981 to 1989, Barbara Pierce Bush served as First Lady of the United States from 1989 to 1993. Rarely has the wife of a president been greeted by the American people and the media with the warmth accorded to the woman who called herself "everybody's grandmother." Her special cause was the promotion of literacy, but she also was an advocate of volunteerism, the homeless, AIDS research, assisting the elderly, and school volunteer programs. (Both, courtesy Grand Hotel.)

Added in 2002, the Jacqueline Kennedy Suite is decorated with interior designer Carleton Varney's individual thematic design, furnishings, and ambiance. Rich, bold blue-and-white striping matches the bedcover to the draperies, with gold accents and lush details throughout. During her lifetime, Jacqueline Lee Bouvier Kennedy Onassis was regarded as an international fashion icon. She was also a symbol of strength for a traumatized nation after the assassination of her husband, Pres. John F. Kennedy, who served from 1961 to 1963 and is regarded as one of the country's most energetic political figures. (Both, courtesy Grand Hotel.)

The Laura Bush Suite was added in 2011 as the seventh Named Room dedicated to a First Lady. Married to George W. Bush, America's 43rd president, Laura Bush is portrayed with a gentle smile and a book on her lap in a painted portrait among the room's tan and gold colors offset by peach and red accents. Born Laura Lane Welch in Midland, Texas, she became known as an advocate for literacy, education, and women's rights. Laura Bush served as First Lady from 2001 to 2009 and often highlighted the importance of preparing children to become lifelong learners. (Courtesy Grand Hotel.)

Grand Hotel also has suites named in honor of two motion pictures filmed at the hotel. The first of these is dedicated to Esther Williams, the swimming champion who received top billing, along with Jimmy Durante, in the 1947 film *This Time for Keeps*. In addition to brightly colored accessories and bedding, the suite is carpeted in a plush aqua base trimmed in maroon. Various framed photographs from filming at the hotel and on Mackinac Island grace the walls, in addition to several theater posters from *This Time for Keeps* and other films in which Esther Williams starred. (Both, courtesy Grand Hotel.)

Perhaps Grand Hotel's best Hollywood link is the 1979 romantic/time-travel love story *Somewhere in Time*. Christopher Reeve, Jane Seymour, and Christopher Plummer became regular fixtures during filming on Mackinac Island in the summer of 1979, and Seymour especially has continued her association through return visits to participate in Grand Hotel's *Somewhere in Time* Weekend, which is held in late October just before the hotel closes for the winter. The suite is decorated in deep blue and red colors and features framed promotional photographs and theater posters. The suite is very much in demand by guests who are enthusiasts of the movie. (Both, courtesy Grand Hotel.)

Five

THE GRAND DINING EXPERIENCE

Upon opening, Grand Hotel immediately established itself as having one of the finest dining rooms on Mackinac Island, rivaling the Island House and the Lakeview Hotel. The Grand Hotel's Main Dining Hall was initially two stories high and used only the finest china and crystal imported from Europe at great expense. Magnificent chandeliers, fine Irish linens, and heavy silverware were part of the visit. Menus were hand-printed every day, and no main dish was served twice during any one week.

Breakfast started with fresh fruit, pastries hot from the oven, and coffee and tea. Next came a variety of egg and meat dishes. Although a luncheon menu was available for midday meals, many guests chose a picnic basket, weather permitting, and took a carriage or bicycle to a lunch destination near the beach or in the woods. However, dinner was a special occasion in itself, with all guests dressed in their finest and meticulously uniformed waiters attending to their every need.

The dinner menus included planked whitefish or trout, dressed lambs, and hot breads served with country butter brought in from a dairy farm in Pickford, Michigan, about 30 miles to the north. Fresh vegetables were served at every meal, followed by special desserts that were as appealing to the eye as to the palate.

Today, Grand Hotel employs a kitchen staff of approximately 100 who prepare as many as 4,000 meals per day. Breakfast and dinner are served from the menu, and the famous Grand Buffet Luncheon offers a variety of dishes in several courses along with salads and designer desserts.

The Grand Hotel's signature dessert is made with vanilla ice cream, the hotel's original fudge sauce, and fresh pecans. More than 6,500 pounds of pecans are used each year to serve approximately 60,000 Grand Pecan Balls per season.

While casual resort clothing is considered appropriate by Grand Hotel standards, prior to 6:30 p.m. the hotel requests a policy of no midriff-baring tops, sweatpants, or cutoff shorts for ladies. For gentlemen, the policy is no sleeveless shirts, sweatpants, or cutoff shorts.

Evenings are indeed a special occasion at Grand Hotel. After 6:30 p.m., dresses, skirts, blouses, dress sweaters, and dress slacks are preferred for ladies, while gentlemen are required to wear a suit coat, necktie, and dress pants, with no denim or shorts. The policy applies to all areas inside the hotel with the exception of the Cupola Bar. Children ages 12 years and older are expected to follow the same dress code as adults.

This early-1900s photograph of the kitchen staff shows a simple operation that even then was expected to provide fine dining to guests of the day. Today's kitchen employs approximately 100, with expectations of food quality and service increased each year. Many employees return to their kitchen positions each season, with some maintaining service records that are decades long. The continuity and quality of service and the food that is served is of utmost importance to Grand Hotel. (Courtesy Bentley Historical Library, University of Michigan.)

The entrance to the Main Dining Hall belies the impressive sight guests will witness upon entering. The fully staffed series of rooms is exquisitely decorated and organized to serve 1,000 guests at breakfast, buffet lunch, or dinner. Upon entering, guests are escorted to their table and immediately offered their beverage choices. Waiters remain nearby to refill water glasses and coffee cups and to attend to any needs diners may have. As many as 20 wine stewards are on duty during dinner, each available to assist a small section of the room. Grand Hotel maintains a strict no-tipping policy that employees reinforce with a smile. (Courtesy Bentley Historical Library, University of Michigan.)

The simplicity of Grand Hotel's early decor is evident in this photograph from an auxiliary dining space off the Main Dining Hall. The chairs, wall treatments, lighting, and room ambiance have undergone many changes over the years. The ultimate comfort of each guest is taken into consideration along with providing serving room for the dining staff who must attend to each diner's needs as they arise. (Courtesy Bentley Historical Library, University of Michigan.)

Pictured here is an early buffet arrangement for a reception featuring a light dinner with hors d'oeuvres and desserts. Entrée servers are stationed at each corner of the buffet, and diners approach an ice sculpture in the middle of the outside tables. Visible on the center table are plenty of desserts ready to be moved into place as the meal progresses. (Courtesy Bentley Historical Library, University of Michigan.)

Grand Hotel's Main Dining Hall seats 1,000 guests and serves three meals per day. Each season, more than 83,000 pounds of prime rib, 23,500 pounds of ham, 83,500 pounds of potatoes, 3,000 pounds of carrots, 14,000 pounds of strawberries, and 6,500 pounds of pecans are served to Grand Hotel's dining guests. All of the deliveries come to the island by ferry and are brought to the hotel by horse-drawn dray. (Courtesy Grand Hotel.)

As in other areas of the hotel, the decor and color themes are often updated, as evidenced when comparing this photograph to the one above it. The influence of designer Carleton Varney cannot be underestimated. Furnishings and wall treatments are all part of the big picture of the hotel's meeting rooms, guest rooms, dining areas, and public spaces. (Courtesy Grand Hotel.)

As if the vibrant colors and excitement of a five-star dining experience are not enough, tables along the front wall of the Main Dining Hall offer window seating that can add incredible views to an already extravagant meal. Usually set in tables for two, the front porch, geranium boxes, and the Straits of Mackinac all come into view, depending on the guest's location. Seating for larger groups is open near the east end of the room with views out a variety of window angles. The sunny daytime feel of the Main Dining Hall transforms into a totally different, elegant ambiance during the evening hours. The dinner menu is renowned for its range and excellence, with three rotating menus throughout the season. Each meal includes a variety of options, beginning with an appetizer and followed by soup, salad, entrée, and dessert. (Both, courtesy Grand Hotel.)

Grand Hotel's well-stocked wine cellar offers many domestic and imported choices, including Michigan brands and the award-winning Grand Hotel Mackinac Island wines that come from the Trinchero Family Estates vineyards in Napa Valley, California. The house wines include sauvignon blanc, pinot noir, chardonnay, cabernet sauvignon, and more and are served in the Main Dining Hall and all of the hotel's properties, including the Woods Restaurant and the Jockey Club. A variety of fresh fruits, gourmet cheeses, spreads, and rolls are also available as starters for a dinner in the Main Dining Hall. (Both, courtesy Grand Hotel.)

Approximately 60,000 Grand Pecan Balls, the hotel's signature dessert since the 1940s, are consumed each season. The base of the pecan ball is creamy Hudsonville vanilla ice cream, which is coated by pecan pieces toasted in a low-heat oven, then applied to the ice cream ball and immediately placed in a freezer. A secret recipe of Mackinac Island fudge sauce is prepared fresh each day in a giant kettle and poured into Grand Hotel's custom-made silver ice cream dishes, which wait in a cooler until the inevitable dessert order comes in. The pecan ball goes straight from the freezer into the dish of fudge sauce and to the guest's table. All Grand Hotel dining properties serve the pecan balls, and Sadie's Ice Cream Parlor offers a mini version. (Courtesy Grand Hotel.)

The dessert menu in the Main Dining Hall includes an impressive array of temptations in addition to the Grand Pecan Ball. Among the favorites are raspberry crème brûlée, the warm chocolate brownie served with black cherry ice cream, salted caramel cheesecake, white chocolate panna cotta and roasted pineapple, and cherry brioche bread pudding served with vanilla sauce. A selection of Hudsonville ice creams are also available, notably double chocolate almond, Mackinac Island fudge, strawberry, and lemon sorbet in addition to creamery blend vanilla. (Courtesy Grand Hotel.)

A timeless tradition for more than 100 years, afternoon tea at Grand Hotel takes place each day in the hotel's parlor. In the mid-1800s, afternoon tea became popular in elite circles, in work environments, and in homes as an activity to break up the day and provide a snack between lunch and dinner, which, in those years, was usually served much later than it customarily is today. (Courtesy Grand Hotel.)

The afternoon tea tradition is enjoyed daily at Grand Hotel between 3:30 p.m. and 5:00 p.m. in the hotel's parlor. Guests sit down and enjoy tea, sherry, champagne, petite finger sandwiches, freshly baked scones, and an array of pastries. Among the decadent delights are tiny cucumber sandwiches, scones the size of a silver dollar, mini tartlet shells filled with fruit and meringue, and strawberries dipped in dark chocolate. The gathering is accompanied by a live music recital. No reservations are necessary, and both hotel guests and visitors are invited. (Courtesy Grand Hotel.)

Conventions, conferences, and social organizations often utilize Grand Hotel's comprehensive food and beverage capabilities to create the perfect setting for an outdoor reception on the porch. Summer on Mackinac Island allows for many afternoon or evening possibilities to socialize, network, and get to know others with generous servings of food and drink nearby. The hotel staff's attention to detail makes these occasions more than memorable, with the classic rocking chairs and million-dollar scenery always at hand. (Both, courtesy Grand Hotel.)

The flexibility of Grand Hotel's hospitality can extend to almost any situation, as shown in this photograph of a picnic arrangement that took place in the ground-floor lobby area. Events of this sort are routinely held outdoors, but inclement weather or other considerations can lead to a change in plans. The hotel's vast array of equipment, supplies, and personnel make thinking outside the box a reality for any organization seeking the perfect location to gather, entertain, or conduct business. (Courtesy Bentley Historical Library, University of Michigan.)

Named for the Mussers' much-loved Scottish terrier, Sadie's Ice Cream Parlor features Grand Hotel pecan ball ice cream inspired by the hotel's signature dessert and made using Michigan's own Hudsonville ice cream. The frozen treats are a perfect way to celebrate a summer afternoon, a bicycle ride, or a walk around Grand Hotel's gardens. Sadie was awarded Best in Show, among other honors, at the 2010 Westminster Dog Show. (Courtesy Grand Hotel.)

Six

RECREATION AT THE GRAND

Grand Hotel encourages guests to exercise and stay physically fit. The Vita Fitness Course on the grounds tests various levels of stamina, strength, and flexibility.

Guests can rent bicycles, walk trails, or go horseback riding nearby. Various lawn games are often underway on the grounds in front of the hotel, including children's events.

Perhaps the most popular activity is playing golf on the hotel's manicured par 67, eighteen-hole course, the Jewel. Of the approximately 15,000 golf courses in the United States, only the Jewel involves a mile-and-a-half horse-drawn carriage ride between nines. The original, shorter front nine features incredible views of the Straits of Mackinac and beautiful tees, fairways, and greens. The newer back nine, the Woods, offers a more modern course design and stunning views of the Mackinac Bridge and the Upper Peninsula. Golf carts can be used on either section of the golf course, but riding one on the village's streets carries a hefty fine, as police will enforce Mackinac Island's ban on motorized vehicles. The carriage ride from the 9th hole is included with the greens fee, and it takes just 15 minutes to get to the 10th tee.

A dip in the Esther Williams Swimming Pool is not only a pleasant way to cool off on a summer afternoon but an activity that has been enjoyed by guests for at least 100 years. One hundred barrels of cement arrived on the island to begin construction of the pool in the spring of 1920, according to a newspaper report. The 220-foot-long serpentine pool was used as a location for the film *This Time for Keeps,* with about one-third of the movie shot on Mackinac Island and at Grand Hotel in 1947 with Jimmy Durante, Xavier Cugat, Lauritz Melchior, and Johnnie Johnston. Williams, a champion swimmer, starred in the romantic comedy—one of several "aquamusicals" that combined her beauty with her swimming talents. The pool was subsequently named after Williams.

For some, the serenity of the picturesque island calls for no more exercise than a stroll on Grand Hotel's front porch or perhaps a leisurely session in one of the porch's rocking chairs.

In this vintage photograph, the pasture in front of Grand Hotel had been purchased and converted to a nine-hole golf course. The foursome includes two women, one of whom is teeing off as the group watches. The fact that women were playing golf attests to the group's elite status at this private golf club. Golf was an activity for those especially well-to-do, as private clubs were in the majority, and public courses had yet to become common. (Courtesy Bentley Historical Library, University of Michigan.)

Pres. Gerald Ford, a Michigan native and the only president to experience Grand Hotel while in office (as of 2020), particularly enjoyed playing golf when visiting the hotel. During his stay on the island, he also played tennis; walked among the gardens with his wife, Betty; and visited a local fudge shop. Ford first visited Mackinac Island in 1929 as a member of the inaugural Fort Mackinac Scout Honor Guard and stayed in the barracks behind Fort Mackinac. (Courtesy National Archives.)

The Jewel, the hotel's golf course, features the original nine-hole course near town and is complemented by nine more holes a mile and a half away in the island's interior. The Jewel has many picturesque locations on the front nine—like this spot overlooking the seventh green—vdespite a less than traditional layout compared to the back nine. Water hazards and forest growth combine with magnificent views of the hotel, the Straits of Mackinac, and the Mackinac Bridge. Golf carts are allowed to be used on both nines of the Jewel, but players will not be in the same cart on both halves of the course. When golfers are ready to play the back nine, known as the Woods, they must take a leisurely 15-minute carriage ride to a location in the middle of the island. The cost of the carriage ride is included in the greens fee. (Courtesy Grand Hotel.)

Lawn games have been part of the guest amenities at Grand Hotel since the grounds began to evolve following construction. In this early-1900s photograph, a sizable crowd has gathered to enjoy a makeshift ball game of sorts featuring hotel employees. The woman "at bat" appears to be using a tennis racquet. (Courtesy Bentley Historical Library, University of Michigan.)

Today, the use of the grounds in front of the hotel can involve lawn games that include bocce ball and croquet. Both sports were quite popular when Grand Hotel opened in 1887. Equipment is available free of charge at the pool house and is suitable for children as well as adults. A recent addition to the lawn games collection involves custom-made Grand Hotel cornhole sets, with beanbags and boards available upon request. (Courtesy Grand Hotel.)

More athletic activities at Grand Hotel are provided at the tennis courts located next to Cadotte Avenue near the flower gardens. At one time, these were the only clay courts in northern Michigan, and they now have an all-weather clay-based surface. Pickleball has also been added and is available on the only clay pickleball court in Michigan (as of 2020). Sports celebrities visiting Grand Hotel may work out or enjoy a game of golf or tennis. The hotel has hosted Arnold Palmer, Dick Vitale, Darrell Waltrip, Roger Penske, Joe Theismann, Jesse Owens, Mary Lou Retton, Jim Nantz, and Ernie Harwell, along with plenty of Detroit Red Wings, Tigers, Pistons, and Lions. (Courtesy Bentley Historical Library, University of Michigan.)

At the Woods restaurant, open to the public, patrons can not only enjoy a fine meal but also try their skill at duckpin bowling. The one-lane alley is the one of the oldest operating duckpin bowling alleys in the United States. Located a short, scenic horse-drawn carriage ride into the interior of Mackinac Island, the Woods provides a casual dining experience. Before or after dinner, another attraction is the freshly popped popcorn and drinks at Bobby's Bar. (Courtesy Bentley Historical Library, University of Michigan.)

The Esther Williams Swimming Pool, constructed in 1920 and most recently remodeled in 2020, is a favorite guest location on a summer afternoon. The 500,000-gallon, serpentine-shaped pool is 220 feet long and heated. The pool area has a large lawn area suitable for sunbathing, with pool equipment and games available for checkout at the pool house. A complete exercise facility is located adjacent to the swimming pool. (Courtesy Grand Hotel.)

Guests need no equipment or specialized clothing to utilize the Vita Fitness Course, located near the greenhouse beyond the pool area. A series of challenges is set up at various stations along the half-mile outdoor course designed to test all skill levels in stamina, strength, and flexibility. The layout is placed along a path of wood chips among shade trees—a welcome relief on a hot or windy day. (Courtesy Grand Hotel.)

As the quickest way to get around on Mackinac Island, riding bicycles remains a traditional transportation choice from the 19th century, when lessons were offered at Grand Hotel to help guests learn to ride. Today, the hotel rents bicycles from the pool house or the Jockey Club, depending on the season, and there are many bicycle rental shops downtown on Main Street. Singles, tandems, and children's bicycles are available to rent by the hour. (Courtesy Grand Hotel.)

A variety of 20 classic carriages from Grand Hotel and Mackinac Island Carriage Tours are on display at Grand Hotel's stables at no charge to the public. Several have been extensively restored to "good as new" condition despite being more than 100 years old. Others were once owned by the Vanderbilt, Woodfill, and Musser families. (Courtesy Grand Hotel.)

Grand Hotel's horses spend the winter at farms in Mackinaw City and Pickford, Michigan, where they are well fed and sheltered from the weather. It is easier to take the horses to their food than it is to bring the food to the island for the horses. They ride a special enclosed ferryboat to the island each spring and to the mainland each fall. Their summer feed supply arrives, and the stables are readied for the horses' return, about one week before the hotel opens. Grand Hotel harnesses Percherons and Hackney horses to its carriages. While on the island's paved streets, the horses wear special polyurethane horseshoes designed for better traction. The horses get haircuts, baths, and individual harness fittings to afford them time to acclimate to the sights and sounds of the island before starting work each season. (Courtesy Grand Hotel.)

Some of the carriages used by Grand Hotel were manufactured more than 100 years ago. Maintenance on these vehicles begins each fall when replacement parts can be ordered—or, more often, fabricated in-house. Each horse's harness is taken apart, cleaned, and oiled in the fall so that worn parts can be repaired or replaced, then re-oiled and reassembled in the spring. The working stables are free to the public and always entertaining to visit. (Courtesy Grand Hotel.)

Seven

HOLLYWOOD AT THE GRAND

Two major movies and several smaller-scale productions have been filmed on Mackinac Island. Grand Hotel had starring roles in the two Hollywood movies.

In 1946, Metro-Goldwyn-Mayer (MGM) Studios cast Esther Williams in her third "water ballet" musical, titled *This Time for Keeps*. Inspired by a 1944 travelogue produced by James Fitzpatrick, MGM producer Joe Pasternak decided that Mackinac Island would make a better backdrop for the film than his original choice of Florida. His crew came to Mackinac in February 1946 to get winter scenery shots of the downtown area, the docks, the Stewart Woodfill residence, and the island's wooded trails. The crew then filmed interior scenes and a few exteriors at MGM Studios' Culver City, California, location using some of the island scenery as backdrops. In July 1946, the principal actors came to Mackinac to film scenes at Grand Hotel and its swimming pool, downtown, and at the coal dock. More than 200 people were hired as extras to appear in the scenes filmed on the island. *This Time for Keeps* was released in 1947.

In 1978, Universal Studios hired Richard Matheson to write a screenplay based on his romantic fantasy novel *Bid Time Return* for a motion picture to be called *Somewhere in Time*. Although the book was set at San Diego's Hotel del Coronado, producers found that hotel too modernized to serve as the locale for the film. Grand Hotel easily filled the need for the required early-1900s ambiance, and although its realism extended to not yet having air-conditioning in 1979, the shooting was completed in July. The story starred Christopher Reeve as Richard Collier, a Chicago playwright who becomes obsessed with a woman he believes he loved in 1912 and attempts hypnotism and time travel in an effort to find her. Jane Seymour was cast as Elise McKenna, the actress who performed at the hotel and was Collier's lost love. The pairing of Seymour and Reeve as a romantic couple still captures the hearts of lovers who enjoy the charisma they brought to their roles.

Pictured are two of the posters used by MGM Studios to publicize *This Time for Keeps* in 1947. One of the songs from the film, "When It's Lilac Time on Mackinac Island," had been composed two years earlier for a short feature about the island and led to Mackinac being used as the setting for the film. About one-third of the 90-minute movie is set on Mackinac Island. While a number of exterior shots and all interior scenes set on the island were filmed at MGM Studios in Culver City, California, multiple outdoor scenes were shot on the island. These included winter footage of the docks, downtown, the Stewart Woodfill residence, and wooded trails. These were filmed in February 1946, with some shots using doubles to represent the principals. Most of the principal cast—including Esther Williams, Johnnie Johnston, Jimmy Durante, and Lauritz Melchior—came to Mackinac Island for several weeks in July 1946 for scenes shot along Main Street, at the coal dock, in front of Grand Hotel, and at the hotel's swimming pool. (Both, courtesy MGM Studios.)

Esther Williams and Jimmy Durante enjoyed star status while they were on Mackinac Island filming *This Time for Keeps* at Grand Hotel. This publicity photograph was taken aboard the ferry *Straits of Mackinac* as it was en route to the island from Mackinaw City. An arrival shot in the movie was filmed on a Hollywood set resembling the deck of the ferryboat with the actors waving to those on shore. (Courtesy MGM Studios.)

Johnnie Johnston (left), Esther Williams (seated at center), and Jimmy Durante posed for this photograph upon their arrival at Grand Hotel by carriage. Guests visible in the background are admiring the celebrities, who drew crowds everywhere they went on the island. Durante's distinctive gravelly speech, Lower East Side accent, comical misuse of language, jazz-influenced songs, and prominent nose helped him to become one of America's most familiar and popular personalities from the 1920s through the 1970s. (Courtesy Grand Hotel.)

Johnnie Johnston and Esther Williams are pictured in a studio shot. Johnston, a baritone crooner, entertained in the 1930s, 1940s, and 1950s as a nightclub, radio, and film singer. He was one of the first artists signed to the fledgling Capitol Records label in 1942. The Stewart Woodfill House was used for exterior shots of the family home of Williams's character in the film. The interiors were all filmed at MGM Studios in Culver City, California. (Courtesy MGM Studios.)

Child actress Sharon McManus and Johnnie Johnston posed for this photograph at the pool (which was later named for Esther Williams) with some of bandleader Xavier Cugat's drums. Multiple songs from the film became popular: "S'no Wonder They Fell in Love" and "When It's Lilac Time on Mackinac Island," along with "Daisy Bell (A Bicycle Built For Two)," which was written in 1892. (Courtesy Grand Hotel.)

Approximately 200 people were hired to work as extras in *This Time for Keeps*, with many of them shown here at Grand Hotel's pool. Esther Williams appeared in swimming scenes filmed at Mackinac Island and at a location in Florida, but when the Florida scenes were blended with shots of her lounging on the lawn at Grand Hotel's pool, the magic of Hollywood makes it appear like she is always swimming at the island. Williams returned to the hotel in 1987 to help the resort celebrate its 100th anniversary, and the hotel named the pool in her honor. (Both, courtesy Mackinac State Historic Parks.)

Esther Williams wore nine specially designed swimsuits in the film, including the "lumberjack-style" suit made of flannel pictured above. Williams said in her autobiography, *The Million Dollar Mermaid*, that she was barely able to keep her head above water due to the weight of the heavy fabric and had to shed the suit in the pool. A teenage swimming champion who set a record for the 100-meter breaststroke in 1939, Williams won a spot on the 1940 US Olympic team. However, the games were cancelled that year due to the outbreak of World War II. (Both, courtesy Grand Hotel.)

English stage and film actress Dame May Whitty, known for her many acting roles and generous charity work, is pictured with Jimmy Durante in a Grand Hotel scene from *This Time for Keeps*. As with many other scenes, the filming of this took place in a studio but was set on Mackinac Island. From the time of the Great Depression through World War II, Grand Hotel fell victim to the lean years of limited travel in the United States. The hotel's business dropped by 90 percent, and at one point, there were 400 employees on staff to serve only 11 paying guests. The film is said to have helped put the hotel back on the road to profitability with a substantial increase in bookings thanks to its visibility in the movie. (Courtesy MGM Studios.)

Grand Hotel owner W. Stewart Woodfill (left) greeted Esther Williams and Jimmy Durante at Mackinac Island as they were set to begin filming *This Time for Keeps* in 1946. Williams considered herself a swimmer rather than an actor yet starred in a number of the "aqua musicals" that were popular at the time. She was an ardent supporter of the sport of synchronized swimming that her films helped popularize. (Courtesy Grand Hotel.)

This image was used on the cover of a collector's edition DVD released in 2000 for *Somewhere in Time*, starring Christopher Reeve, Jane Seymour, and Christopher Plummer. A number of factors dampened the movie's chances for early success, including a low promotional budget and a premiere held at Grand Hotel on Mackinac Island—not a Hollywood or New York opening with lots of publicity. It grossed only $1.2 million dollars during its opening weekend in 1980. An actor's strike prohibited any of the principals from attending the premiere or appearing on talk shows to plug the film, which only ran in theaters for three weeks. Grand Hotel won out as the film's locale after San Diego's Hotel del Coronado, where the book's story took place, was judged by producers to be too modern. (Courtesy Universal Studios.)

This original theater poster for *Somewhere in Time* was used in promotional materials during the first 20 years of the film's existence. Panned by critics, *Somewhere in Time* cost $5.1 million to make and only grossed $9.7 million. It seemed lost to the B-movie archives until cable television movie channels and the advent of video cassette players allowed it a second chance as a video-store rental. Soon, it was regarded as a cult classic. (Courtesy INSITE.)

In 1979, *Somewhere in Time* was filmed at various locations on Mackinac Island, with much of it taking place at Grand Hotel. Christopher Reeve (shown in the scene when he first arrives at the hotel's front porch), Jane Seymour, and Christopher Plummer starred in the romantic story of a playwright's time travel in search of a woman he loved. The film became a cult classic and generated a yearly weekend celebration at the hotel featuring period dress and visits from cast and crew members. (Courtesy Isidore Mankofsky.)

Christopher Reeve, as Richard Collier, appears lost in thoughts of Elise while enjoying lunch in Grand Hotel's Main Dining Hall. The film's set decorators used the modern decor of the room for scenes set in the present day, but the creation of the 1912 look had to wait until dinner had finished at 9:00 p.m. The window dressings, lamps, walls, and chairs were all changed to create an aura of the past. Filming took place until 5:00 a.m., when everything had to be taken down and the dining room returned to its modern look in time for breakfast guests. (Courtesy Universal Studios.)

Actor Christopher Reeve gets a quick makeup refresher before shooting a scene in front of the Haunted Theater in downtown Mackinac Island. Fresh off his success as the star of *Superman*, Reeve had on-screen chemistry with Jane Seymour that earned legions of fans who reveled in the romance created by their characters. Reeve acted as Richard Collier in many contentious scenes opposite Christopher Plummer, whose character William F. Robinson confronted Collier over his interest in Elise McKenna, played by Seymour. In the film, Robinson was the manager of McKenna's acting career and dominated her time, career, and relationships. (Courtesy INSITE.)

Richard Collier's 1979 Fiat Spider is ready for a scene on Cadotte Avenue near Grand Hotel, along with a spare car used as a backup. Automobiles are prohibited on Mackinac Island, where transportation is only by horse, carriage, bicycle, or foot. Special permits were required to bring the vehicles necessary for the film's production to the island. Approximately 600 people were hired as extras for parts in the film. (Courtesy INSITE.)

Because of the island's ban on automobiles, the Mackinac Island State Park Commission had to grant permits to allow for the use of five semi-trucks full of props, costumes, cameras, set pieces, and sound equipment for the production. In addition, several cars featured in the film were also granted permission to be on the island. The permitting process is quite strict—they are issued not only by the day but by the hour. Overall, the production was filmed in approximately six weeks. (Courtesy Isidore Mankofsky.)

Universal Studios had a set designed and built with a front desk for the film. It was transported to the hotel by dray and installed in the parlor for the front-desk scenes and redesigned from a 1970s look to 1912 as the production schedule evolved. (Courtesy Universal Studios.)

Christopher Reeve is shown consoling Sean Hayden, who played the part of Young Arthur, son of Grand Hotel's 1912 desk clerk in the film. The hotel's parlor was refurbished to become the lobby, as it had been many years before. The entire decor of the parlor was changed from then-present-day 1979 to 1912. Producer Stephen Deutsch promised Grand Hotel owner R.D. Musser II that the hotel would have a favorable depiction in the film, in essence becoming a "character," in exchange for the free use of the hotel for filming. The agreement saved a substantial amount of money in a production budget that had already been cut in half. (Courtesy Universal Studios.)

Richard Collier first saw Elise McKenna's portrait in the mythical "Hall of History" at Grand Hotel. The ethereal moment convinces Collier that she indeed did perform in a play at the hotel in 1912, and that he must go back in time to find her. Guests frequently ask where the "Hall of History" is at the hotel, but it was pure Hollywood. The set was created solely for the film in a section of the Main Dining Hall. (Courtesy Universal Studios.)

Jane Seymour is shown here in her role as Elise McKenna (with actress Audrie Neenan playing a maid) in the stage play scene in which Elise delivers a monologue about "the man of my dreams." Filming took place in the theater at the Mackinac Hotel and Conference Center across town, later renamed Mission Point Resort. There is a small plaque commemorating the seat where Christopher Reeve sat as Richard Collier while watching the play *Wisdom of the Heart*. Grand Hotel owner R.D. Musser II made Universal Studios producer Stephen Deutsch aware of a production studio and soundstage on the Mackinac Hotel's grounds near the theater. Universal saved $2 million in production costs by using the facility for set construction, housing, costuming, filming interior scenes, and viewing daily footage. (Courtesy Universal Studios.)

Christopher Reeve's character, Richard Collier, spent the night sleeping on a wicker sofa at the west end of Grand Hotel's world-famous porch after being threatened by William F. Robinson, played by Christopher Plummer, to stay away from Elise McKenna. Visitors to the hotel often desire to "live the movie" for a few days during their visit to the site where it was filmed. Grand Hotel's scenery, mixed with the magic of Mackinac Island, has served to encourage visitors who want to relive the romance of the film or re-create it in their own lives. (Courtesy Universal Studios.)

Characterized by many as one of the most romantic kisses in the history of cinema, Richard Collier and Elise McKenna's first affection in Room 117 (the room does not actually exist in the hotel, by the way) begins their long-sought time alone. Later, after a picnic lunch in the room, Collier discovers a current-day coin in his pocket that spoils the 1912 spell he has been under and returns him to the present. (Courtesy Universal Studios.)

A permanent monument in the form of a beautiful plaque commemorating the "Is It You?" scene at the site of Richard and Elise's first meeting at the Mackinac lakeshore was created by the International Network of *Somewhere in Time* Enthusiasts (INSITE) and unveiled in 1993. The monument is located just down the hill from Grand Hotel's pool area and garden greenhouse. A 15-minute walk from the ferry docks, it is on the lake side of the road just beyond the end of the boardwalk, past the school playground. (Courtesy INSITE.)

Jane Seymour, dressed as her movie character Elise McKenna, has returned to Grand Hotel on several occasions to meet with fans of *Somewhere in Time*. Ever gracious, Seymour has brought her family and mingled with guests while dressing the part her fans recall so well. Each October, the hotel hosts an annual *Somewhere in Time* Weekend gathering of the International Network of *Somewhere in Time* Enthusiasts (INSITE). Many attendees dress in vintage 1912 attire to celebrate with the film's cast and crew members. Christopher Reeve and multiple other actors from the film have returned to the island to participate in the weekend's events. INSITE funded Seymour's and Reeve's stars on the Hollywood Walk of Fame and has raised more than $25,000 for spinal cord research in honor of Reeve for the Christopher and Dana Reeve Foundation. Since 1990, INSITE has published a magazine for fans of the film. (Courtesy INSITE.)

Eight

HONORED GUESTS AND ENTERTAINMENT

Entertainment for guests has always been a major part of a Grand Hotel stay. Since the 1800s, guests have enjoyed extravagant activities, and the entertainment has followed suit. Opera stars sang to guests during meals or at evening band concerts. The hotel constructed a balcony above the Main Dining Hall where a 12-piece orchestra played to guests during dinner. The popularity of the orchestras meant that musicians were employed for the entire summer. String bands also set up on the porch to provide afternoon entertainment. Nightly dances were held and continue to this day in the Terrace Room, where the Grand Hotel Orchestra regularly performs.

Lecturers, speakers, and exciting product demonstrations have offered guests options for their evening plans. In 1895, Mark Twain lectured in the Grand Hotel Casino—admission was $1. By 1935, a radio salon was added so that patrons could listen to *The Jack Benny Program*, baseball broadcasts, and other popular shows.

Today, Grand Hotel incorporates many forms of entertainment for the pleasure of its guests. Jazz, classical, and popular music can often be heard in the hotel's theater, dining room, and lounge areas. Conventions and conferences employ national and regional headliners for after-dinner entertainment.

Harry S. Truman was the guest of W. Stewart Woodfill at Grand Hotel in 1955. His visit was part of a fundraising trip for his presidential library after he was out of office. As the 33rd president, Truman served from 1945 to 1953, succeeding from vice president upon the death of Franklin D. Roosevelt. As president, he is credited with making some of the most crucial decisions in history at the end of World War II. (Courtesy Bentley Historical Library, University of Michigan.)

Grand Hotel owner W. Stewart Woodfill hosted John F. Kennedy while the senator was campaigning for president in 1960. Kennedy also posed with Michigan governor G. Mennen Williams on the Mackinac Bridge. Williams and Woodfill had both championed the cause of getting the bridge built in the 1950s. (Courtesy Bentley Historical Library, University of Michigan.)

Although six different US presidents have visited Grand Hotel as of 2020, Gerald Ford (shown above in 1976 with his wife, Betty) is the only president to visit while in office. Others visited while campaigning or prior to or after being elected president. Ford stayed at the Michigan governor's summer residence as the guest of Gov. William Milliken but also spent time at the hotel playing golf and tennis. The Fords attended church services at Trinity Episcopal Church. (Above, courtesy Bentley Historical Library, University of Michigan; below, courtesy Grand Hotel.)

Over the years, Grand Hotel has hosted innumerable celebrity guests and entertainment acts. Six men who became US presidents have visited the hotel, as have several candidates. Senators, governors, mayors, diplomats, and ambassadors have enjoyed Grand Hotel's hospitality and amenities. R.D. Musser II is pictured on the hotel's front porch with Bill and Hillary Clinton during the 1987 Democratic Governors' Conference, hosted by Gov. James Blanchard. Every Michigan governor, senator, or congressman makes it a point to attend political events at Grand Hotel; it is a "must-visit" destination on the campaign trail. (Courtesy Grand Hotel.)

Rev. Jesse Jackson (right) was welcomed to Grand Hotel by R.D. Musser II. The civil rights activist, Baptist minister, and politician was a candidate for the Democratic presidential nomination in 1984 and 1988. Grand Hotel became known as a political mecca, with 23 presidential hopefuls having visited as of 2020. Other high profile politicians who have walked the front porch include Vice Pres. Dick Cheney, Gov. Jerry Brown, Sen. Susan Collins, Gov. Mario Cuomo, Gov. Michael Dukakis, Rep. Newt Gingrich, Justice Ruth Bader Ginsburg, Sen. Al Gore, Justice Sandra Day O'Connor, Sen. Robert Dole (and his wife, Elizabeth Dole), Vice Pres. Alben W. Barkley, Gov. Thomas E. Dewey, Vice Pres. John Nance Garner, Gov. John Kasich, Sen. Carl Levin, Sen. Debbie Stabenow, Gov. Mitt Romney, Gov. Pete Wilson, Gov. George Voinovich, Gen. Colin Powell, and many, many more. (Courtesy Grand Hotel.)

Pres. George H.W. Bush visited Grand Hotel on several occasions, but all of them were before or after he served as the 41st president of the United States from 1989 to 1993. While attending a Forbes conference in 2005, Bush was greeted at the hotel's front door by Mackinac County sheriff Scott Strait (pictured with Bush), who assisted Secret Service agents with Bush's security team. The affable Bush was accompanied by Steve Forbes, who was hosting the event, and Bush took the time to chat with Strait and then introduced him to Forbes. "It was one of the best moments in my life," said Strait. (Courtesy Scott Strait.)

In 2019, Vice Pres. Mike Pence became the first sitting vice president to visit Grand Hotel. Pence spoke at the Republican Governors' Conference and traveled in a motorcade of eight SUVs to and from the Mackinac Island Airport, raising the ire of island purists who believed that the ban on automobiles applied to all and that this was disrespectful to local tradition. Others pointed out that the Secret Service had quietly brought a backup car to the island when Gerald Ford visited as a sitting president in 1976, "just in case." Ford traveled everywhere on the island by horse-drawn carriage. (Courtesy IN.gov.)

Salisbury's Famous Concert and Dance Orchestra is pictured in what might be one of the oldest photographs of musicians at Grand Hotel. Instruments visible in this 10-piece ensemble include drums, string bass, trombone, cornet, violins, viola, cello, flute, and clarinet. It is possible that the two ladies could have been vocalists performing with the group. (Courtesy Bentley Historical Library, University of Michigan.)

Another musical group competing as one of the earliest to play at Grand Hotel could be this ensemble gathered on the west end of the porch with a sizable crowd behind them. The lineup looks very similar to the Salisbury band above, but these clearly are not the same musicians. The absence of one string player is one of the few differences in the instruments used by this unidentified group. (Courtesy Bentley Historical Library, University of Michigan.)

Posing on the Grand Hotel lawn for a photograph are Charles L. Fischer and His Globe Trotters, who prided themselves on having traveled "twice around the world." In 1926, Fischer's band of Kalamazoo musicians contracted with Belgium's Red Star Line for a four-month around-the-world cruise as the official shipboard orchestra aboard the SS *Belgenland*. The group was so successful that it was subsequently engaged for three more world cruises; the always-busy band appeared in this photograph during a break between its second and third cruises. (Courtesy Bentley Historical Library, University of Michigan.)

Musical combos, like this jazz sextet, have often entertained at various Grand Hotel functions. Grand Hotel hosts an annual Jazz Weekend each Labor Day, featuring jazz music played by some of the country's top performers. The series has welcomed musicians including Dave Brubeck, Eartha Kitt, George Benson, Herbie Hancock, Pete Fountain, Ramsey Lewis, Chuck Mangione, Manhattan Transfer, Herbie Mann, the Preservation Hall Jazz Band, and Branford, Jason, and Wynton Marsalis. (Courtesy Bentley Historical Library, University of Michigan.)

Larger musical groups take the stage in Grand Hotel's theater, which is capable of seating bigger crowds for dinner and shows. The saxophonist is taking the lead in this jazz ensemble's piece, with a trumpeter ready for the next section of the song. The acoustics of the theater are excellent and provide great sound for the audience no matter the genre of music. (Courtesy Grand Hotel.)

In the Terrace Room, a standard evening's entertainment is provided by the Grand Hotel Orchestra. A great place to spot celebrities visiting Grand Hotel, the Terrace Room provides a nightclub atmosphere that draws those looking for an evening of dancing and tunes. It would not be unusual to see other musicians relaxing here, including Pat Boone, Mel Torme, the Four Tops, Marie Osmond, Tito Puente, Boots Randolph, the Four Freshmen, Lou Rawls, Kenny Loggins, Madonna, or Kid Rock, all of whom have visited Grand Hotel. (Courtesy Grand Hotel.)

More intimate venues like the Audubon Wine Bar can feature a solo pianist for a relaxing evening of enjoyment. An excellent, comfortable place for conversation, the hotel has been the ideal spot for guests including Dr. Joyce Brothers, Steve Forbes, Alex Haley, Lee Iacocca, astronauts Jim Lovell and Jerry Linenger, and Bishop Fulton J. Sheen. (Courtesy Grand Hotel.)

This trio was perfect entertainment for a reception held in Grand Hotel's theater. Likely tasked with being "wallpaper" for the reception, which undoubtedly had the attendees in conversation the entire time, the trio's placement on stage gives it visibility for those wanting to still be able to hear the musicians despite the din of those talking. (Courtesy Grand Hotel.)

Author Mike Fornes performed as Gordon Lightfoot in concert at Grand Hotel's theater for the 2017 Michigan Bankers Association Convention. In addition to keeping up his concert schedule in seven states and Canada, Fornes often leads tour groups on summer excursions around the Mackinac area, including at Grand Hotel. (Courtesy Sundown Productions.)

Students from the theater department at Michigan State University (MSU) have performed as part of the Grand Hotel Arts Weekend, presented by the Michigan State University College of Arts and Letters. The MSU Musical Theatre Touring Company performs Golden Age show tunes as part of an annual event schedule that includes performances showcasing theater and music. (Courtesy Grand Hotel.)

Actress Esther Williams returned to Grand Hotel in 1967 to help celebrate its 100th anniversary with the Musser family, who are seated with her next to the pool. Pictured here are, from left to right, Williams; Daniel Musser II and his wife, Amelia; Marlee Brown Musser; and Daniel Musser III. Other celebrities who have visited include Dan Blocker, Rosemary Clooney, Jeff Daniels, Robert De Niro, James Earl Jones, Jim Nabors, Debra Winger, Hugh O'Brien, Kate Upton, and Jerry Van Dyke, among others. (Courtesy Bentley Historical Library, University of Michigan.)

Flip Wilson kept the audience in stitches with his comedy act, later changing into drag to perform as his famous character Geraldine. From 1970 to 1974, Wilson hosted his own weekly variety series, *The Flip Wilson Show*. Television personalities who came to Grand Hotel include Hugh Downs, Barbara Walters, Chris Mathews, Greta Van Susteren, Mike Rowe, Paul Harvey, and Bill O'Reilly. (Courtesy Bentley Historical Library, University of Michigan.)

Comedienne Phyllis Diller performed at Grand Hotel's theater to the delight of a full house. One of the first female stand-up comics, Diller's self-deprecating humor brought her a lengthy career performing in nightclubs, television, and movies. From the world of comedy, Grand Hotel has also welcomed George Goebel, Jack Benny, and Rich Little, to name a few. (Courtesy Bentley Historical Library, University of Michigan.)

Nine

BEHIND THE SCENES

To attain the level of quality that Grand Hotel ensures for every guest, a tremendous amount of work goes on behind the scenes thanks to a large staff of personnel who mostly go unseen. In addition to the dining room servers, groundskeepers, and bellmen who present more of a public face to visitors, there are housekeepers, cooks, office personnel, and maintenance workers who, although they are mostly invisible to the public, play key roles in a guest's visit. Some of their work is done during the height of the tourist season (July and August are peak times), and other tasks begin once the last guest goes home in the fall and continue until the first guest arrives the next spring (the hotel is open from May 1 to October 31).

The public's perception may be that Mackinac Island goes to sleep in the winter, and that Grand Hotel is closed up and dark. The hotel is technically closed for the season, but plenty of work goes on during this time, and the island is busy in a quiet sort of way.

Maintenance and construction take place all winter. Workers cover every piece of parlor furniture. Housekeeping personnel remove all linens and bedding before they depart for the season. In recent years, more than 1,000 pieces of furniture have been removed from 200 guest rooms. Sixteen bathrooms have been renovated.

The work is continuous right up until opening day during the following spring. Larger projects are completed well in advance, like the remodeling of the west end of the world's longest front porch that called for removal of all the original wood—right down to the foundation—and reconstruction of the framing with a nonskid sealing on the surface. Other chores may seem mundane but are important. For example, there are 535 fire extinguishers on the property that must be inspected every year and certified as ready for service.

The housekeeping department begins preseason preparations about six weeks before the hotel opens. Every area of the hotel is deep-cleaned, including guest rooms, public spaces, and hallways. All of the lights, chandeliers, drapes, valances, and canopies are washed. The flooring is scrubbed, and all carpets are cleaned.

Beginning in late March, the season's supplies begin to arrive. It takes about three weeks for coolers, freezers, and dry storage to be filled. This includes all of the inventories of the hotel shops, room amenities, and the initial food orders for the employee cafeteria, where up to 300 meals are made per day for staff and contractors beginning April 1. The supplies first arrive via ferry and are then transported to the hotel by horse-drawn dray, often filling the receiving dock several times each day.

Grand Hotel serves as many as 4,000 meals per day, seven days a week, and employs a kitchen staff of approximately 100. The team prepares breakfast and dinner as ordered from the menu as well as the famous Grand Buffet Luncheon with a variety of hot and cold entrées, seafood, and a selection of meats in several courses along with salads and designer desserts. Fresh desserts are crafted daily in the kitchen's extensive preparation area. (Both, courtesy Bentley Historical Library, University of Michigan.)

Grand Hotel's kitchen has every sort of appliance needed for the preparation of quality food, including massive ovens for baking. The staff does an incredible job of constantly cleaning and sanitizing each and every utensil, plate, cup, and cooking instrument on a per-use basis. Cold and hot entrées, salads, finger foods, meat and seafood dishes, fresh fruits, side dishes, and desserts are prepared each day to the highest levels of culinary excellence. Whether it is as simple as a vegetable tray or an order of the famous Grand Pecan Balls, the veteran staff strives to provide deliciousness to guests with the utmost care and presentation. (Above, courtesy Bentley Historical Library, University of Michigan; below, courtesy Grand Hotel.)

Grand Hotel operates on a seasonal basis, generally opening on May 1 and closing on October 31. After guests depart, construction workers arrive to begin maintenance, remodeling, and redecorating as needed. Major projects are completed during the island's winter season despite limited ferry access and severe weather conditions. The Esther Williams Swimming Pool has been renovated several times, most recently in 2020. The process involves bringing specialized equipment to the island to complete the job before the snow flies. Long before winter even hints at arriving, horses begin to depart Mackinac Island by ferryboat for their off-season homes in Mackinaw City or Pickford, Michigan. By the time the transfers are complete, only a dozen or so horses remain on the island out of the approximately 500 that worked there all summer. (Both, courtesy Grand Hotel.)

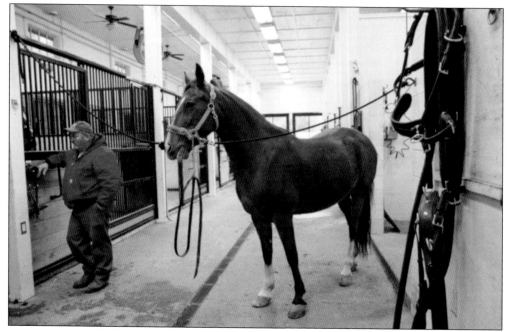

The water tower, which supplied all the hotel's needs, stood for decades and appears in many photographs. When a reconstruction and upgrade eliminated the need for the tower, workers disassembled the structure in the off-season and demolished it. Winter provided the perfect time for the job in terms of safety and going unnoticed by visitors. What was once a landmark on the island was no longer needed, and the view of the hotel from the front immediately improved. Progress allowed for enhancement of the scenery. (Both, courtesy Bentley Historical Library, University of Michigan.)

Off-season maintenance and repairs can range from work on the front porch pillars to the portico that covers the stairs at the main entrance. Tasks of this nature are accomplished during the winter season, when the hotel is closed to guests. These photographs from 1977–1978 were taken during a major reconstruction of the foundation under the front porch. The degraded timbers that had been in place for more than a century were replaced with steel and concrete, assuring a solid base for another 100 years. (Both, courtesy Bentley Historical Library, University of Michigan.)

Indoor winter work at Grand Hotel would provoke a double-take from guests used to the beautiful settings during the summer season. The above photograph shows a remodeling project, with flooring, support columns, and walls being inspected and replaced. The below photograph was taken during a major reconstruction of the theater. A new stage was constructed in addition to a new ceiling and backstage amenities to support the variety of acts performing at Grand Hotel. When rooms and office space have been added or a dining room remodeled at Grand Hotel, the work has often taken the entire winter season to complete, weather permitting. (Both, courtesy Bentley Historical Library, University of Michigan.)

Preparing Grand Hotel for another season begins before the winter snows are gone—about six weeks before the hotel opens around May 1. Each room is deep-cleaned and dusted, with furniture uncovered, and all items are polished and inspected. Every light and appliance is checked for reliability, and replacements are made before the first guest arrives. The Musser family has always personally seen to this. It is done every year to assure the absolute best first impression possible for guests arriving at the hotel. (Courtesy Grand Hotel.)

This vintage photograph of the bellman crew shows the incredible detail that goes into the fashions of the bellmen and the uniformity of their presentation. A bellman's job at Grand Hotel encompasses far more than arranging luggage transfers and horse-drawn taxi services. They are expected to know every aspect of the hotel's services and cater to any guest's request or answer questions about the hotel or Mackinac Island. (Courtesy Bentley Historical Library, University of Michigan.)

With more than 150,000 overnight guests each season, Grand Hotel has a staff that remains invaluable. The human resources department is very busy during the winter months as they work to hire the right candidates to fill positions throughout the hotel before the doors open in May. In the weeks prior to the hotel's opening, employees are brought up to speed on their roles at Grand Hotel as they fill out new-hire paperwork, attend orientation, receive uniforms, and are assigned housing. The hotel also helps employees adjust to island living by assisting them with essentials such as locating the post office, medical center, and grocery store. Grand Hotel has 15 shops with a staff of 48 who come from all over the world. Working with more than 500 vendors, it takes 8 to 10 people three weeks to unpack, price, and display all the merchandise before the season begins. (Courtesy Jim Addie.)

Ten

A HISTORICAL
PERSPECTIVE

From 1933 through 2019, the Musser family preserved the history and tradition of Grand Hotel, constantly improving the experience of every guest for more than 85 years.

W. Stewart Woodfill started working at the hotel as a desk clerk in 1919 and bought the Grand Hotel in 1933. Woodfill's nephew R.D. Musser II began working for him in the bar in 1951, while he was in college. R.D. Musser II then moved to the kitchen, and by 1960, he had moved up to president, eventually purchasing Grand Hotel with his wife, Amelia, in 1979.

R.D. and Amelia's son Dan Musser III started working at the hotel while he was in high school, raking sand traps on the Jewel. He then worked as a bellhop, bartender, front desk clerk, front desk manager, reservations manager, and vice president, He became president in 1989.

Each owner has been very hands-on, bringing their own improvements and maintaining the hotel's ambiance while changing with the times and embracing technology.

Marketing a first-class hotel entails many aspects of doing business with the traveling public, from initial bookings and enticing repeat customers to developing group sales strategies and hosting themed events.

The early days of Grand Hotel involved railroads and steamship lines having a place to take passengers, albeit only for the summer season. Through the years, the clientele included the very well-to-do, the elite business traveler, the conventioneer, families, the curious, and prominent guests from the political, entertainment, and corporate worlds.

Themed events have provided an element of excitement and glamour for the hotel's parlor, grounds, and amenities. The *Somewhere in Time* Weekend spurred other ideas that work in conjunction with the atmosphere and aura of Grand Hotel. Some modern events include Halloween Weekend, Labor Day Jazz Weekend, Titanic at the Grand, Arts Weekend, Ballroom Dancing Weekend, the Grand Garden Show, Murder Mystery Weekend, Wine Appreciation Weekends (for summer and fall), the popular Old Fashioned Mackinac Fourth of July Celebration, and a Grand Princess and Superhero Package to delight children.

Across three centuries, Grand Hotel has been guided by a very small corps of owners concentrated into three generations of families in modern times.

W. Stewart Woodfill was associated with Grand Hotel for more than 50 years after starting there in 1919 as a desk clerk. He eventually became manager, and in 1925, he and two partners bought the hotel. He sold his share in the property to his partners in 1927, two years before the stock market crashed, and in 1931, Grand Hotel went into receivership. At a March 1933 bankruptcy auction, Woodfill himself was the sole bidder. He became the new owner during the bleakest year of the Great Depression, nursed Grand Hotel through the 1930s, and survived World War II in spite of a cut in consumer travel. Woodfill operated the hotel until 1979, when he sold it to his nephew and successor, R.D. Musser II, five years before he died. (Courtesy Grand Hotel.)

From 1933 through 2019, the Musser family has preserved the history and tradition of Grand Hotel, thoughtfully improving the Grand experience of every guest for more than 85 years. In October 2019, a new chapter began for Grand Hotel as Pivot Hotel and Resorts, the luxury division of Davidson Hotels and Resorts, took over the management for owner KSL Capital Partners. R.D. Musser II, pictured here with his wife, Amelia, passed along the Musser family legacy at Grand Hotel to their son Daniel Musser III, who remains as chairman and works closely with his sister Mimi Cunningham. (Courtesy Grand Hotel.)

R.D. (Dan) Musser III is now chairman of Grand Hotel. Along with his sister Mimi Cunningham, Musser represents the third generation of Musser family ownership and operation of Grand Hotel, the world's largest summer resort. Under the new ownership of KSL Capital Partners, Musser remains responsible for all day-to-day operations, which include overseeing the front desk, convention services, food and beverage, sales and marketing, housekeeping, maintenance, and recreation. Musser started full time at the hotel in 1986 and worked his way up through every department to gain a thorough understanding of all aspects of running the business. He served as a kitchen assistant, bellman, bartender, bar manager, front desk clerk, front desk manager, reservations manager, and vice president. He was named president in 1989. Active in the hotel industry, Musser is the former chairman of the Michigan Hotel, Motel, and Resort Association and former chairman of the resort committee of the American Hotel and Lodging Association. (Both, courtesy Grand Hotel.)

The world's longest front porch, at 660 feet long, is indeed a wonder to behold. An early edition of *Ripley's Believe It or Not!* tried to lengthen it, claiming it was 680 feet long, but truth be told, it is long enough to be one of the greatest relaxation places on earth. There are many comfortable rocking chairs along Grand Hotel's front wall and 260 porch flower boxes—filled with seven tons of soil and 2,500 geraniums—that provide a perfect accent for guests whether they are rocking or socializing while gazing at a million-dollar view of the Straits of Mackinac. A vendor on a bicycle offers soft drinks to those on the porch, and the Geranium Bar, located just inside, will happily deliver a favorite libation directly to one's rocking chair. There is a giant-sized chess set waiting to be played and musical entertainment in the evening, weather permitting. It does not get any better than summertime on Grand Hotel's front porch. (Courtesy Grand Hotel.)

Grand Hotel's new management group, Davidson Hotels and Resorts, took over in 2019 and committed to significant improvements, beginning with employee housing. Team members are an integral part of Grand Hotel's culture and guest experience, and upon their return to Mackinac Island in late April 2020, they found updated accommodations throughout approximately 70 percent of the employee buildings. The updates include new floors, paint, decor, full Wi-Fi access, and a fitness facility. Also new in 2020, many Grand Hotel shops were completely replaced with brand-new looks, and Grand Coffee and Provisions made its debut as a casual dining option offering grab-and-go breakfast and lunch items for guests. The Esther Williams Swimming Pool underwent a complete remodeling in 2020 and reopened in 2021. (Courtesy Grand Hotel.)

Discover Thousands of Local History Books Featuring Millions of Vintage Images

Arcadia Publishing, the leading local history publisher in the United States, is committed to making history accessible and meaningful through publishing books that celebrate and preserve the heritage of America's people and places.

Find more books like this at
www.arcadiapublishing.com

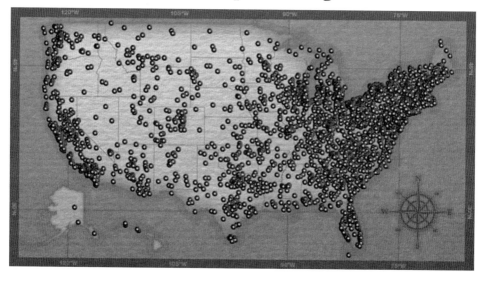

Search for your hometown history, your old stomping grounds, and even your favorite sports team.

Consistent with our mission to preserve history on a local level, this book was printed in South Carolina on American-made paper and manufactured entirely in the United States. Products carrying the accredited Forest Stewardship Council (FSC) label are printed on 100 percent FSC-certified paper.

MADE IN THE USA